Brain Training for Kids with ADHD

101 Fun Exercises and Logic Puzzles to Improve Focus, Concentration, Self-Regulation, and Executive Functioning Skills

Table of Contents

Introduction Letter to Parents

Dear Parents,

In front of you is a comprehensive book packed with brain-exercising activities for children with ADHD. Attention Deficit Hyperactivity Disorder, commonly known as ADHD, is a neurodevelopmental condition affecting social, emotional, and educational aspects of life. This book addresses the most common issues children with ADHD face, including the inability to focus, memorize things, handle intense emotions, organize their lives, and build and maintain relationships.

This book addresses your child's physical, emotional, and mental challenges by equipping them with the tools they need to overcome their issues and navigate the world. By working through these activities, your child will learn skills they can apply throughout life, empowering them to grow into confident and productive adults. Moreover, the exercises will lay the foundation for learning through fun, a proven way to help children acquire essential life skills.

Introduction Letter to Children

Hey Kids!

Do you know the feeling when you're supposed to complete a task and can't focus, no matter how hard you try? You know that by not finishing it on time, you'll miss out on doing something fun, yet you can't make yourself concentrate. The harder you try, the more your thoughts seem to go in different directions, making you upset, angry, and frustrated.

If this sounds familiar to you, don't worry – you aren't alone! Many other children and adults struggle with this, but there is help for everyone. This book will help you beat distractions through playful activities you can do alone or with your parents, friends, or family. Each exercise is fun and easy to complete, yet completing them will teach you how to cope with hardships without feeling like it's the end of the world.

By helping you explore your strengths and weaknesses and teaching you how to build the skills you need to overcome your challenges, this book will show you how to go through life in a different, better way. Once you've learned these skills, you can use them whenever necessary, even when you're all grown up!

Section 1: Unraveling ADHD

ADHD is a condition that causes people to lose focus and control over their emotions and actions. It's a unique way of thinking and experiencing the world - it's called being neurodivergent. It doesn't make you worth less than a neurotypical person (someone who doesn't have ADHD). For example, you may take longer to finish your homework than your siblings or classmates because you have to work on focusing on it more.

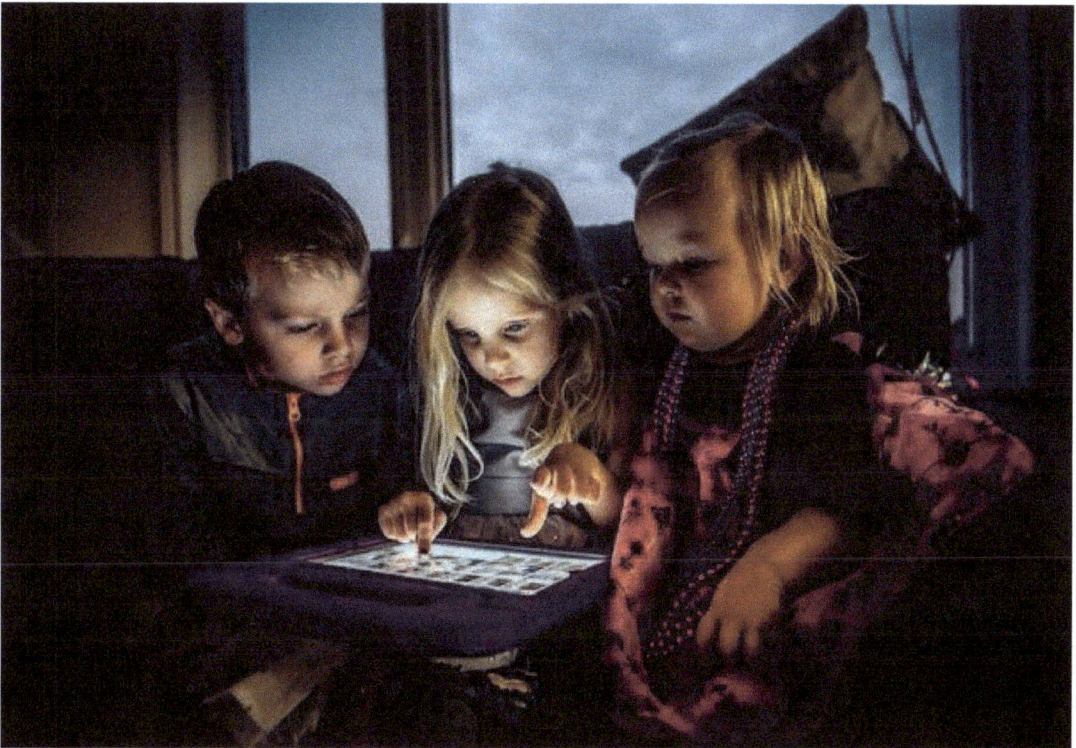

You may take longer to finish your homework than your siblings or classmates because you have to work on focusing on it more.
https://www.pexels.com/photo/three-children-looking-at-a-tablet-computer-3536480/

However, ADHD can affect much more than school assignments or homework. It can also make you procrastinate on home chores and cause you to struggle to make friends because you can't control your intense emotions. Despite all these negatives, ADHD is a manageable condition. People who have it can live happy and successful lives. It's all a question of learning to manage your symptoms and coming up with the best strategies to overcome your difficulties.

When learning how to cope with your condition, you need to know what type of ADHD you have. Here are the main types:

- **Inattentive and Distractible:** People with this type aren't hyperactive. They lose focus easily and are distracted by everything and everyone around them.

- **Impulsive and Hyperactive:** Those with this type are too active and often act without thinking but have no trouble focusing.

- **Combined:** This type combines the other two and causes short attention span, impulsivity, and hyperactivity.

THE 3 ADHD-TYPES

mostly Hyperactive – Impulsive

ADHD -HI

Aliens are what most people think of when they hear ADHD.

They're Hyperactive in talking or movement, impulsive and are always looking for new paths in life. Emotions can boil up fast as they are very passionate!

They might blurt out one or two inappropriate things in their fight against injustice.

(also ADHD-PH)

mostly Combined

ADHD - C

Is probably the most "confusing" type, as they show Symptoms from both sides, not really belonging into one category.

Not being quite "Hyperactive enough to fit the stereotype, this ambiguity might be why they have a hard time realizing they have ADHD.

mostly Inattentive (formerly "ADD")

ADHD - I

Can be the hardest to detect due to the lack of visible Hyperactivity.

In fact, they might appear to move unusually slow, as they try to deal with their hyperactive mind. This makes them amazing observers. They might not notice when being talked to, but will notice even the most trivial things. (also ADHD-PI)

Whichever form of ADHD you have, you're much more than the challenges you experience. Each type comes with unique strengths and abilities, too. You can think of these as superpowers to unlock. With a little bit of love and positivity (and the exercises below), you can use them to your advantage and rise above your challenges like a superhero rises above the villains.

Exercise 1

Determine whether the statements are true or false to learn more about ADHD. Check the answer key below to see how many answers you get right.

1. ADHD is a medical condition a person can learn to live with.
2. ADHD is a serious mental health disorder or disability.
3. ADHD doesn't define who you are today or who you'll grow up to be.
4. If you have ADHD, you can never be as smart as other children or do as well in school.
5. You can overcome ADHD if you behave better.
6. Your parents can help you overcome difficulties.
7. You have ADHD, so you can get away with bad behavior.

A) True - You can absolutely learn to live with your condition.

B) False - ADHD affects everyone differently. It's not a disability or a mental health disorder. Your brain is just wired differently.

C) True - You don't have to let your condition define you.

D) False - By focusing on your strengths and learning to overcome your weaknesses, you can do just as well in school as those without ADHD.

E) False - Changing your behavior forcibly won't help overcome the thinking and emotional issues you're facing.

F) True - Your parents are your best allies when managing ADHD.

G) False - Having ADHD is not an excuse for poor behavior, although it can get you into trouble at times.

Exercise 2

This exercise is called *"What are my ADHD Traits?"* It requires you to select the challenges you experience the most so you can learn how to combat them. Put a checkmark in front of the issues you remember having lately.

- Trouble focusing on a task for a long period of time.
- Trouble focusing on others when they're talking to you.
- Getting distracted by sounds, smells, and sights.
- Trouble focusing on details, like finding the differences between two pictures.
- Forgetting things you're supposed to do or say.
- Can't organize schoolwork or your room and lose things.
- Difficulty learning anything new and having poor grades.
- Interrupting others.
- Being impatient - can never wait for your turn.
- Doing and saying things without thinking.
- Blurting out answers without waiting to be asked.
- You're always on the move, even if you don't have to go anywhere.
- Struggling to sit or stand still.
- Squirming and fidgeting whenever forced to sit for long.

Exercise 3

Here's a *"My Superpowers"* activity to discover your strengths. Check the skills you think you're good at.

- Having a lot of energy and never feeling tired
- Bouncing back easily after facing challenging emotions or situations
- Being a creative thinker
- Focusing intensely on what you enjoy doing
- Being brave and unafraid of taking risks
- Being honest and helpful
- Knowing how to have fun
- Know when you're facing big emotions, even if you don't know how to cope with them

Exercise 4

Say It Out Loud is a fun activity that teaches you to focus and describe what you're doing or want to do. When doing a task (whether it's homework, a household chore, or anything else that requires attention), say what you're about to do out loud. Start doing it, and repeat your reminder several times if you find yourself getting distracted. Each time you do, make a mark on a piece of paper. When finished, look how many times you had to remind yourself. It shows you how many times you got distracted.

Exercise 5

Music can also help you learn more about your ADHD. If you love music, listening to your favorite songs during non-school-related activities (music would be distracting when doing homework) can motivate you to stay on task. Music helps your brain organize tasks and improve its ability to learn and remember things. You can also sing or make up a dance when cleaning or tidying your room. Dancing is also a great way to burn off excess energy if you have hyperactive ADHD.

Exercise 6

Number games like Sudoku can improve your skills in combating ADHD.

Wegge at the Danish language Wikipedia, CC BY-SA 3.0 <http://creativecommons.org/licenses/by-sa/3.0/>, via Wikimedia Commons: https://commons.wikimedia.org/wiki/File:Sudoku_grid_onlypos.png

Number games like Sudoku can improve your skills in combating ADHD. Place the numbers 1-9 on a grid as shown above. Insert the numbers in each square, column, and row without repeating them within the row or column. You can find numerous Sudoku games online with different difficulty levels and test your abilities. Start with the easiest one and practice it until your focus and memory skills improve.

Exercise 7

Modeling (acting like) your parents is another excellent way to learn about everyday challenges. They might not face the same issues as you, but they also have difficulties. Ask them how they resolve their problems. What do they do when they feel overwhelmed, frustrated, or impatient? Do they have a go-to technique for pausing and letting go of negative emotions and thoughts?

Exercise 8

Learning how to remain calm wins half the battle. While this is easier said than done, whichever type of ADHD you have, it will be easier to manage if you don't let your emotions overwhelm you. A great technique is to find a quiet space to calm down whenever you experience a challenging situation. When you get to this space, start inhaling while counting to 3, then exhale while counting to 3 again.

Repeat until you feel your body and mind relaxing.

Exercise 9

Creating a schedule you can stick to will do wonders for your ability to practice the important skills and overcome ADHD challenges. Knowing you'll do something you enjoy after a frustrating task will motivate you to push through. Create a list of must-dos followed by fun activities, and you'll soon see the benefits. You can write your list in the space below.

MY CHORES

NAME:

CHORE

	SUN	MON	TUE	WED	THU	FRI	SAT
	☐	☐	☐	☐	☐	☐	☐
	☐	☐	☐	☐	☐	☐	☐
	☐	☐	☐	☐	☐	☐	☐
	☐	☐	☐	☐	☐	☐	☐
	☐	☐	☐	☐	☐	☐	☐
	☐	☐	☐	☐	☐	☐	☐
	☐	☐	☐	☐	☐	☐	☐
	☐	☐	☐	☐	☐	☐	☐
	☐	☐	☐	☐	☐	☐	☐
	☐	☐	☐	☐	☐	☐	☐
	☐	☐	☐	☐	☐	☐	☐
	☐	☐	☐	☐	☐	☐	☐
	☐	☐	☐	☐	☐	☐	☐
	☐	☐	☐	☐	☐	☐	☐
	☐	☐	☐	☐	☐	☐	☐
	☐	☐	☐	☐	☐	☐	☐

Exercise 10

Now that you've figured out your strengths and weaknesses, it's time to embrace them as part of yourself. To do this, repeat to yourself at least once a week that your experiences are *normal* even though they might differ from other children's. Acknowledge your differences by saying them out loud.

Exercise 11

Learn more about how your brain works. The internet has a lot of information - use it to learn how your brain works and why it functions differently than some other kids' brains. When you have this information, try to connect it with your experiences. At least once a week, think back to challenging situations and try to find their reasons. What can you learn about your own brain?

Bonus Learning Box: Here is more information on what to do when feeling overwhelmed or needing additional help managing ADHD symptoms:

Break school - and homework into smaller chunks

Ask your parents help to organize your room and school bag

When doing homework or any other task that requires attention, sit away from other children, doors, windows, etc.

Take short breaks during tasks that require sitting and focus; get up and move, take a walk, play with a pet...

Be active when not doing tasks that require sitting and focusing

Eat healthy food - too much sugar can make you both hyperactive and drowsy

Get enough sleep - don't use gadgets at nighttime as they could make it harder for you to fall asleep

Section 2: Brain Training: Why Do I Need This?

You probably heard how physical activity is great for exercising your muscles and keeping fit. Did you know that you can exercise your brain, too? This is what brain training activities do:

- They help you build and strengthen thinking (cognitive) abilities like focus, memory, and sharper thinking.

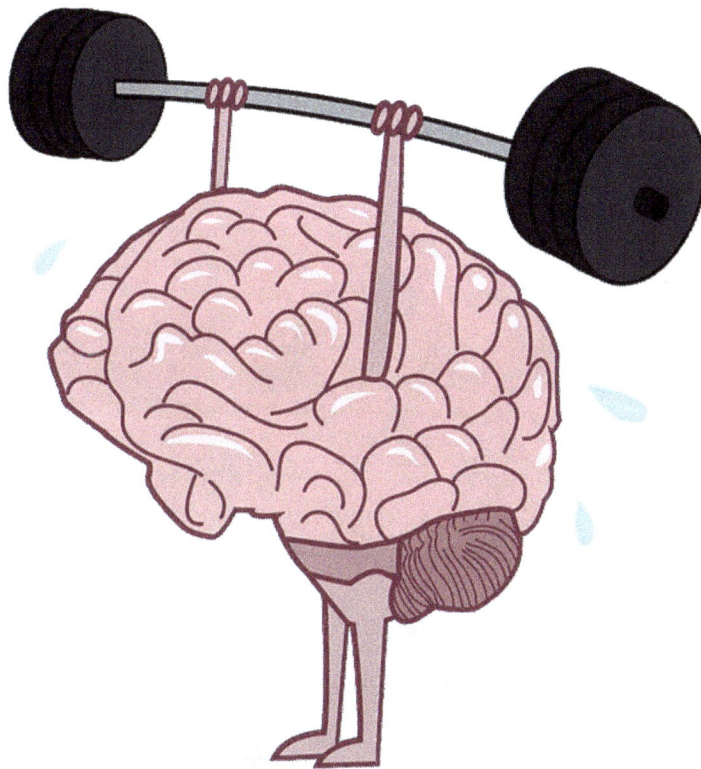

Brain training activities help you build and strengthen cognitive abilities like focus, memory, and sharper thinking.
https://pixabay.com/illustrations/brain-exercise-training-5983810/

"A mind in motion is a sign of growth and intelligence." - Unknown

- When your brain is better at directing your thoughts and not letting itself get distracted, it helps you control your emotions. Brain training is a great way to learn about big feelings and how to cope with them.

If you ever tried rubbing your belly in a circular motion while patting your head at the same time, you know how challenging this simple exercise can be! Yet, it teaches you to focus on what you're doing and keep up with two different movements. Over time, the brain starts remembering what it's supposed to, so it will come naturally to you.

"Knowledge will bring you the opportunity to make a difference." - Claire Fagan

Building Legos or completing jigsaw puzzles are also brain-training activities. With both, you must pay attention, remember your previous moves and where things go, plan your next moves, and get creative. However, for any exercise to work efficiently on your brain, *you must do it consistently.*

Exercise 12

Red Light - Green Light is a group activity that helps you with tasks that require movement. One person stands across the room and acts as the traffic light, saying red or green light, signaling the other person(s) to stop or go. The other players start walking across the space, and when the traffic light person tells them to stop, they should stop. If they don't, they must return to where they started.

Exercise 13

The Head - Shoulders - Knees and Toes game (with a little twist) is another brain exercise. Instead of pointing to the body parts in the song's lyrics, you can switch up the meanings. Write down the changes, and practice them. For example, when the song says ears, you can point to your head instead – but you have to do it that way every time! When it says shoulders, you point to your chest, etc., it makes your brain work a little harder, improving how well it works!

When the song says ears, you can point to your head.
https://commons.wikimedia.org/wiki/File:Marines_teach_English_to_Okinawa_students_through_song,_play_during_new_program_140919-M-PJ295-342.jpg

Exercise 14

Drum Beats is for music lovers. Adding rhythm to an activity improves your focus, and you won't be distracted as easily. You'll need a small drum (or something that can substitute as a drum) and at least one more player. One person plays the drum, and the other(s) do certain movements. For example, to one beat, they open their arms. To two beats, they clap. They do a jumping jack to three beats, and to four beats, they start walking.

Exercise 15

You can play the *Giant Dwarf* game with family or friends. One person stands and waits for another to say either giant or dwarf. When the person yells "Giant!" the person standing rises on their tiptoes to appear as tall as possible. When they say "Dwarf!" the other person drops to their haunches to look as small as possible.

Exercise 16

The classic *Where is the Ball* game needs a small ball and three cups. Ask someone to hide the ball under one cup and switch up the places of all three cups several times. Pay close attention to the cup hiding the ball to see where it ends up. Guess where the ball is.

Exercise 17

COPY THE PICTURE

Draw in the empty grid to create the same shape as you see on the left grid.

Exercise 18

Even looking for items on a list can be a great brain teaser. Ask a parent to create a list of items in a room (it could be your room, the kitchen, etc.) Take the list and let the scavenger hunt begin. Try to find as many items as possible from your list and check them off as you go.

Exercise 19

Color sorting is another activity guaranteed to exercise your brain. Get plenty of building blocks or other small toys in different colors. On a piece of paper, write down how many are red, blue, green, and so on.

Exercise 20

Design your own scavenger hunt game by creating 5-6 clue cards. Ask someone to place them across your room or wherever you play. If the first one says, "Look under your chair," the second one should be placed under your chair, etc. Then, the one found under the chair sends you to a third location and another hint. Use a treat in the last place; this will help you *want to complete the hunt*, looking for all the clues until you find your prize.

CLUE CARDS
for a scavenger hunt

Clue # 1 will soon be found, all you have to do is turn around!

Hooray! You're almost there! Look for the next clue under your chair!

A story that teaches a lesson may be called a fable. Find the next clue under the table.

Clue # 6 Looking for the next direction? Go to the place you see your reflection.

Here's clue # 4! The next place opens and shuts. Go look by a door!

Don't get frustrated! Don't get grumpy! Just search for the next clue by someone's cubby.

Looking for the missing link? Just take a look by the sink.

To wash your hands you simply need warm water, paper towels and soap.

Exercise 21

If you like to dance but can't focus during organized classes, have a dance party at home. Plan a themed party and ask family or friends to join you. It's a great chance to fish out those Halloween costumes, as they'll make the party even more special! Dance at your own rhythm and burn off that restless energy while having fun.

Section 3: My Focus and Attention

Attention is a unique skill that can be developed and strengthened through brain training and practice. This is necessary because it's an ability often affected by ADHD. For example, if you have inattentive or combined ADHD, you can easily lose focus on what you're doing.

Attention is a unique skill that can be developed and strengthened through brain training and practice.
https://pixabay.com/illustrations/banner-header-attention-caution-1165978/

Have you ever found yourself suddenly thinking of what you'll do after a class while you were still in class – and were supposed to be listening to the teacher explaining something? Maybe you were asked to sit quietly when visiting relatives but couldn't stop fidgeting. Both are examples of problems with attention. In the first case, you're distracted by your own thoughts. Secondly, you can't focus on sitting quietly and moving impulsively.

A girl named Diana had a similar problem. Whenever talking to her friend in school, she found herself thinking about what she wanted to eat when she arrived home. When the friend asked her a question, she couldn't answer because she had no idea what the friend was talking about. Her friend got upset, and Diana was frustrated because she didn't do it on purpose! To work on her short attention span, Diana started practicing a brain exercise called *mindfulness.*

Mindfulness trains your brain to be more aware of what you're doing so it won't get distracted by thoughts or impulses. In Diana's case, mindfulness helped her shut out everything else when talking to her friend so she could listen more attentively.

Besides mindfulness, there are several other ways to stay focused. You'll find a few suggestions listed below.

Exercise 22

The easiest way to work on your focus is to play games where you need to find a hidden object.
Muband at Japanese Wikipedia, CC BY-SA 3.0 <http://creativecommons.org/licenses/by-sa/3.0/>, via Wikimedia Commons: https://commons.wikimedia.org/wiki/File:Spot_the_difference.png

The easiest way to work on your focus is to play games where you need to find a hidden object. Look at the image above. Can you spot the differences?

Exercise 23

9	3	6
5	8	2
7	4	1

Look at the grid and find two numbers that make 10 when added together (like 5+5, 3+7, etc.) Find as many pairs as possible. Cross out the numbers you paired, and repeat until you've found all the pairs.

Exercise 24

Playing with memory cards is another way to improve your focus. Lay out the cards face up (creating pairs) and try to memorize them. Turn them face down and start turning them face up two at a time to find pairs. Start practicing with 6-8 cards at first and slowly work towards memorizing more and more cards.

MEMORY CARD GAME

Exercise 25

As a more challenging alternative to the previous memory card exercise, you can lay out the cards face up and try to remember as many of them as possible. Then, ask someone to gather the cards, add additional ones, and start showing them to you one by one. Guess whether you've seen the card before or not to test and improve your attention.

Exercise 26

Jigsaw puzzles test your concentration.

Classic puzzle games, like a simple jigsaw puzzle, are the ultimate test of concentration because they force you to pay attention to where the pieces go and how to put together a picture to make it whole.

Exercise 27

Paddleball is a game that combines focus and movement. Start practicing by bouncing the ball downward. You'll have to focus on not losing the ball and letting it move only between the paddle and the floor. When you've mastered the downward bounce, start bouncing the ball up in the air.

Exercise 28

Combining relaxation and positive imagery is a mindfulness technique designed to improve focus and help a person learn new skills. To use this method, think about a situation when you are most likely to get distracted or act impulsive. Then, imagine not letting your thoughts or behavior get out of your control in the same situations. For example, if you can't pay attention during class, visualize paying attention the entire time. Your brain learns these responses and teaches you to remain alert.

Exercise 29

The Coin Game will boost your attention and concentration. Find a piece of cardboard and a pile of different coins; you'll need around 20. Choose six coins from the pile and lay them out in a row. Look at them carefully, then cover them with cardboard. Start a timer on a kitchen timer (ask mom) or on your cell (if you have one), and try to make the same coin row using the remaining coins in the pile. When you've finished, stop the timer and reveal the hidden sequence. Write down if you created the same sequence and how long it took you to do it. If you weren't successful, cover the sequence and try again.

Exercise 30

Following audio instructions makes searching for items on a list even more challenging. Have someone use a voice recorder (on a cell phone) to say a list of items for you to find. Listen to the recording and start hunting!

Exercise 31

Create brain break cards for different situations for what to do when feeling overwhelmed. For example, if you find yourself distracted while doing homework, draw a brain break card and do whatever the card tells you to do. This could be getting up and walking to the kitchen or doing a quick mindfulness exercise like deep breathing. This exercise will help you let go of the unhelpful and distracting thoughts.

Section 4: Memory Mastery

ADHD is directly linked to forgetfulness and poor working memory. It causes a person to have a hard time concentrating and remembering to do tasks or chores. The main reason behind this is that ADHD affects *executive functioning skills.* You need these abilities to do well in school, at home, or in social circumstances (like talking to friends)). The good news is brain training can help you improve these skills by working on the different parts of memory, such as recalling, working memory, and organization.

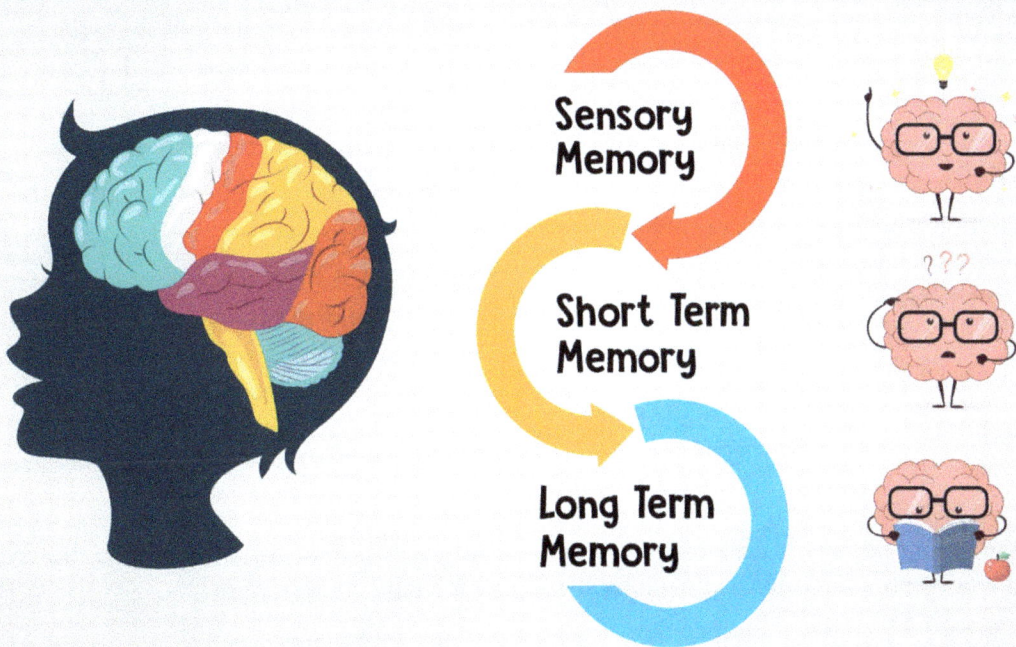

3 TYPES OF WORKING MEMORY

Sensory Memory

Short Term Memory

Long Term Memory

The special skills can be *regulatory* and *organizational*. The first ones include decision-making, controlling your feelings, focusing on how you experience everything around you, and starting an action. All of these affect your memory because they impact how your brain works. *Organizational* skills help gather information about regulatory skills.

Memory has different forms. For example, *working memory* is the one you use every day to remember things your brain stores in different parts of your mind. *Short-term memory* allows you to remember information for a short period, like when you're asked to bring your plate from the table to the sink after dinner. Working memory helps this process along, boosting your short-term memory.

Long-term memory remembers information after a long period of time. For example, when you learn to ride a bike, this information is stored in your long-term memory. You can stop riding for weeks or months (even years), but you'll still remember how to do it next time around.

Memory challenges can hurt your performance at school when taking tests or notes or trying to memorize information you read in a book or hear from a teacher. However, there's help for this! There are ways to study and ways to manage memory hurdles in the classroom. Some suggestions for this are:

- Games that require focus and problem-solving improve working and short-term memory.
- Try memory tools designed to boost long-term memory, like reminders, to learn more.
- Use reminders for important tasks to stay on top of your assignments.
- If you struggle with short-term memory, do *only one task at a time*.
- Be physically active, as exercise improves your brain's functions.

Exercise 32

The Pizza Memory game is simple – but it's an incredible help to keep you motivated. Draw a large pizza (filled with only sauce). Then, create cut-outs of toppings like pepperoni, cheese, chicken, pineapple, etc., separately. Cut these items out and place double-sided tape on the bottom of each topping.

Now, draw several pizzas with different toppings already on them and cut these out, too.

Now, grab one of the finished pizza pictures, look at it, then set it aside. Try to recreate that pizza by sticking the right toppings onto the empty crust.

Exercise 33

In the *Suitcase Game*, one player tells everyone what they would put in a suitcase. The others must remember this list, and then a second player repeats it and adds a new item to the list. The third does the same, and so on. Each player has to remember what all the other players added to the suitcase – and the list grows!

Exercise 34

Place 20 items on a tray and look at them carefully. Cover the tray with a large piece of paper and try to remember the items you saw on the tray. Set a timer for 30 seconds and write down as many items as you can recall seeing. Uncover the tray to see how many you got right.

Exercise 35

Yoga is a great way to activate memory. Sit on the floor with your legs crossed. Make a fist with your right hand and stick out your thumb. While holding it, make a fist with your left hand and stick out your pinky. Without looking at your hands, change the finger positions by sticking out your pinky on the right and sticking out your thumb on the left. Keep doing this until it becomes easier!

Exercise 36

With some creativity, you can make your own memory card game. Cut out 20 card-sized papers and write one word on each (use words for everyday objects, animals, etc.). Lay out six cards and memorize the words they contain. Shuffle the cards with the others, then ask someone to start picking cards one by one. Your goal is to identify whether the word you see on the cards was among the six ones you saw before.

Exercise 37

During the *Memory Jar* activity, you can play a fun game for a longer time. For example, you can create memory jars for vacation, the school year, or the summer you spend playing with friends. Each day or week (depending on how long the period lasts), write your favorite memory on a small piece of paper and place it in a glass jar. At the end of the period, empty out the jar's contents and look back at your favorite memories. Do you remember each one?

Exercise 38

To play the *Picnic* game, you must find the following items in your home: fruit (any fruit works), a ball, a hat, ham, cheese, plates, salad, cookies, a blanket, sunglasses, a ball, yogurt, your favorite drink, bread, sunscreen, insect repellent. You only have two minutes to look at this list. Then, gather every item you can remember seeing into a picnic basket. How many did you get?

Exercise 39

Try to recall as many sea creatures as possible.
https://pixabay.com/illustrations/aquarium-fish-fish-tank-sea-life-284551/

Look at the picture above for one minute. Cover the paper and try to recall as many sea creatures as possible.

Exercise 40

To play the *Magic Potion* memory game, write down the ingredients you would put into a magical potion, and feel free to let your imagination run wild. Look at the list for two minutes, then turn the paper face down. Set a timer for one minute. During that time, try to remember as many ingredients as you can. Keep them in your mind and compare your mental list with the actual list.

Exercise 41

Ask someone to read the following out loud (without looking at it yourself):

- Brown boat
- Yellow parrot
- Gray house
- Blue hat
- Red car
- Green frog
- Pink gift
- Purple cake
- Orange balloons

Color the objects below the same colors.

Can you remember the color?
https://pixabay.com/vectors/boat-sailboat-coloring-page-sailing-6769421/

Can you remember the color?

https://pixabay.com/illustrations/parrot-nature-bird-animal-outline-8214921/

Can you remember the color?

https://pixabay.com/illustrations/picture-puzzle-coloring-page-4286688/

Can you remember the color?

Can you remember the color?

Can you remember the color?

Can you remember the color?

Can you remember the colors?

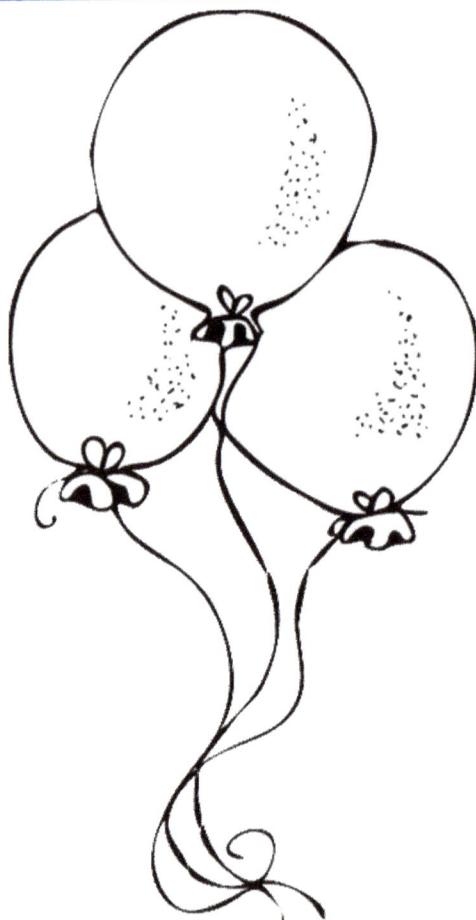

Can you remember the colors?

Section 5: The Big Emotions

People with ADHD experience emotions differently and more deeply, so they often become overwhelmed by them and act out.

Big emotions are very strong feelings that may cause sensations all over your body. They're also more difficult to manage as they can cause you to feel like you're losing control. You might even struggle to describe how or why you feel the way you do because the feelings sneak up on you without warning. These emotions aren't bad, and everybody has them from time to time.

One of the benefits of brain training is that it helps you control and manage big feelings like anger, frustration, sadness, excitement, etc. To understand how this works, you'll first need to explore what emotions are, their use, and their importance in your life.

You need to explore what emotions are, their use, and their importance in your life.

The inability to control big emotions that arise from nowhere is a common issue people with ADHD have. Your friends who don't have ADHD can handle teasing or getting frustrated when something doesn't go as planned by letting go of these feelings, but you can't because your emotions feel more intense.

Exercise 42

Intense emotions can sometimes feel like uninvited guests in your mind. However, as unpleasant as they are, by greeting them with the following *Uninvited Guest Welcome*, you can show them they can't bother you anymore:

This is a guest house that receives new arrivals every day.

Some are unexpected, but I'll still welcome them all.

Even if they make me sad or anxious and threaten to make me lose control,

I'll still treat my guests respectfully.

Because I know they are not forever - and have a purpose.

After dark, there is always light.

By inviting dark emotions, I invite positivity too.

I'm grateful for whatever comes because it helps me get stronger.

Exercise 43

Here is an emotion check questionnaire to help you learn more about your big feelings:

- What emotions do you experience most often?
- Why do you think you have these feelings so often?
- Do you know why they appear when they do?
- Do you deny or try to stomp out your emotions? If yes, how does this make you feel?
- How would you feel if you welcomed them instead?
- Are there any benefits to embracing intense emotions?
- Have you ever felt your emotions become too strong?

Exercise 44

The *Positive Remembering* exercise helps develop the skill of looking back on positive memories from the past and enjoying the positive emotions they bring. Sit in a quiet place and take 10 minutes to recall a memory that makes you feel happy and good about yourself. Try to visualize the memory in as much detail as possible so you can focus on how it made you feel. You're training your brain to keep positive emotions longer, and this helps push out the negative ones.

Exercise 45

Remember, there's always something to be grateful for. Think about what you feel thankful for today or this week, and write it down here so you can reread it when you feel bad:

Exercise 46

Self-compassion teaches you to be kind to yourself when you feel overwhelmed by anger, frustration, sadness, or any other negative emotion. Practicing self-compassion will also help you feel better about yourself and focus on positives instead of negative experiences. Find a quiet place where you can take five minutes to focus on your breathing. Breathe deeply in and out, and place your hands on your stomach. With each breath, remind yourself that while you'll face hard moments, if you accept yourself, nothing else matters.

Exercise 47

Finding the positive side of a negative experience encourages you to look at it as a learning opportunity. Think about a recent negative experience, like when you were frustrated because you couldn't focus on homework or felt uncontrollable anger because someone teased you at school. Answer the following questions:

- How did this experience make you feel?

_____

_____

- Did you notice any feeling now that *you didn't feel* when you first had the experience?

_____

_____

- Did you learn anything from this experience?

_____

_____

- Do you think you'll handle similar situations in the future the same way?

_____

_____

- What could you do to handle these situations better?

_____

_____

Exercise 48

Another way to appreciate your superpowers is to write your life story, including past, present, and future. When doing so, ask yourself the following questions:

- When looking into your past, were there challenges you overcame?

_____

_____

- What strengths allowed you to overcome your challenges?

_____

_____

- Were you able to remain calm, focused, and think before you acted?

_____

_____

- How do you feel about who you are right now?

_____

_____

- Do you have the same challenges?

_____

_____

- Do you use the strengths that helped you in the past?

_____

_____

- Have you discovered new superpowers recently, and how can they help you overcome new challenges?

_____

_____

- How will your future life (including school, home, and spending time with friends) be different from how it is now?

_____

_____

- Do you think you can work on your strengths even more?

_____

_____

- Will you do something differently now?

_____

_____

- What would you like to achieve in the future, and how can you do it?

_____

_____

Exercise 49

At the end of each day, write what enjoyable activities you did alone (like listening to music, reading), with others (like playing a game with your friends), and a meaningful way you were able to help someone else (like sharing your lunch with a schoolmate who didn't have their own).

Exercise 50

You can also ask your parents, relatives, and friends to each write a list of positive qualities they think you have. Reading how they appreciate your effort to overcome your challenges and see you committed to becoming better and happier will surely uplift your day.

Exercise 51

The *Quicksand* game is about conquering one of the most common intense feelings associated with ADHD: anxiety (worrying). To play this game, imagine walking near the desert and suddenly finding yourself in the middle of quicksand! In your mind, see the sand swallowing your feet and think about what you could do now. You'll probably get anxious, but if you want to get out, you must focus on how to escape. Redirect your thoughts toward finding a solution (like grabbing the nearest fixed item). As soon as this happens, you'll feel your anxiety go away.

Section 6: Learning Self-Control

Impulsivity (doing things without thinking) is another big part of ADHD. However, developing better self-control skills and becoming more aware of your impulsive actions will help you prevent them. You can make *intentional* choices instead. Self-control means knowing how to take charge of sudden negative thoughts and emotions that cause you to act without thinking or not in an acceptable way.

Self-control is a group of complex skills that a person develops over time. These include:

- **Emotional** control: Knowing how to remain calm and continue with what you must do when unexpected changes happen or you get upset.

- **Impulse** control: Understanding the need to pause before you say or do something.

- **Movement** control: Knowing when it is appropriate to move around and when to remain still.

Self-control is an *executive functioning skill* that helps you live a better life. It helps you get along with others and learn in your environment. For example, self-control allows you to remain calm even if one of your friends says or does something that upsets you during a game. Using self-control, you'll have enough patience to wait your turn during multiplayer games or wait in line in the grocery store.

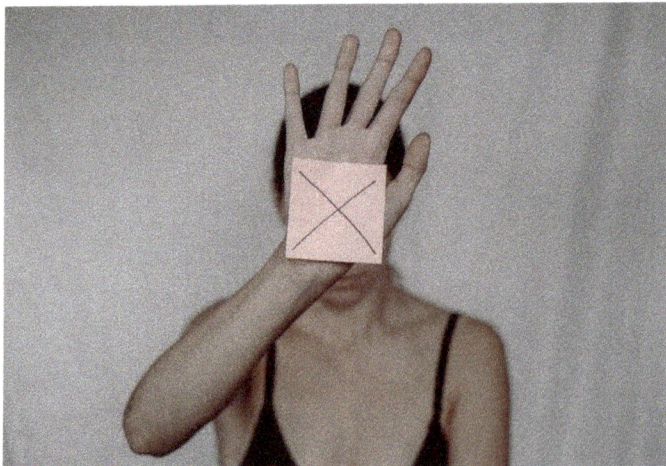

Self-control means knowing how to take charge of sudden negative thoughts and emotions that cause you to act without thinking or not in an acceptable way.

https://www.pexels.com/photo/woman-showing-paper-with-prohibition-sign-5723268/

People with ADHD often get frustrated when they can't cope with their challenges or become impatient when they feel forced into situations they can't handle. Because of this, self-control has plenty of benefits when used in school, at home, or in any social setting.

Exercise 52

A good old-fashioned snowball fight will burn off your excess energy and make you less fidgety and restless when you need to focus on something. Even if you live where there isn't much snow, or you can't wait until winter), you can play the indoor version. To do this, ball up several white socks and put them into a small laundry basket. Get teams together, and let the fun begin!

Exercise 53

Mindfulness exercises teach you how to recognize and accept your impulses.

Instructions:

1. Sit comfortably, let your body relax, and close your eyes.
2. Notice how your chest moves when you're breathing.
3. Breathe in through your nostrils, then breathe out. Continue breathing slowly for a couple of minutes.
4. How do you feel? Does the air tickle your nose when you breathe in and out? Does it feel warm or cool? Do you feel your chest or belly expand more when you breathe in?
5. Notice how much calmer you feel, like nothing could bother you.
6. Do you feel anything else in your body or mind? Perhaps sadness, anger, or any other negative emotions? Where did they come from? What caused them?
7. Think about the negative experience you had recently. When did you first feel angry, sad, or any other intense feeling you identified?
8. Once you learn where the feelings came from, exhale deeply to let them out.
9. Open your eyes and pay attention to how you feel. Are the feelings gone? Even if not, now you know where they came from, so you can do something about it.

Exercise 54

This activity will also help you pause and track impulsive behaviors and their outcomes. Complete the worksheet to find out how.

- When you feel you'll act impulsively, think about what you're about to do. Ask why you're doing it five times and write down each answer. Did the answer change by the fifth time?

_____

_____

_____

_____

_____

- Do you think something bad will happen if you don't act right away? What do you think will happen?

_____

_____

_____

- If you're reacting to something someone else said or did, think about if you do the same thing in the same way. What reasons could they have for saying or doing what they did?

_____

_____

_____

- What happens if you act on your impulses?

_____

_____

_____

- What if you let yourself experience the big feelings but find a different way to cope with them? Would that change the outcome? If yes, how?

_____

_____

_____

Exercise 55

This exercise will help you see impulsive urges when they happen and what triggers them. Ask yourself the following questions when you're about to act out:

- Why do you want to do it?
- Have you thought things through, or are you jumping to conclusions?
- What's behind your behavior? Was your reaction triggered by something someone else said or did?
- How are you feeling, and would acting on your impulse make you feel better?

- What do you believe or think about the circumstance (what happened) that triggered your actions?

- Can you change what you think or believe? If so, would this change your behavior?

- What would others think about your behavior? Would they act in the same way?

- How would they react instead? Would their reaction resolve the problem faster?

Exercise 56

Do you want to learn to make more thoughtful decisions and stop acting impulsively? This activity will teach you how to get into the practice of thinking about the consequences of your actions and whether they are worth it.

1. Start by identifying *physical signs*. For example, do you tend to clench your fist before you act impulsively? Is your heart racing so fast it feels like it will jump out of your chest?

2. Whenever you notice these signs, stop and try to calm yourself.

3. Taking deep breaths will slow your heart and breathing. Breathe while counting to 10.

4. Think about why you want to act impulsively. Is there a problem? If yes, what can you do to solve it?

5. Once you think things through, you'll see that having a clear head makes it easier to make better decisions.

Exercise 57

Swimming is a mindfulness-friendly sport.
https://www.pexels.com/photo/2-girl-s-swimming-during-daytime-61129/

A mindfulness-friendly sport can help you gain control over your impulses. For example, swimming moves your entire body. However, it also makes you feel weightless, removing distractions that hinder your awareness. When swimming, you can become more aware of your thoughts and emotions (so you can identify them).

Exercise 58

Arts and crafts help you express your emotions and learn more about them. Whether it's painting, sculpting, playing music, or any other art form, it will engage your senses and make you aware of your feelings.

Exercise 59

Strength training activities will raise your self-awareness. Start lifting child-sized dumbbells for 15 minutes daily (this exercise will be helpful when you feel restless or need to take a break from tasks requiring focus), and you'll soon see the difference in your control.

Exercise 60

Set goals and rewards for reaching them. For example, you can have a small treat when you don't act impulsively despite feeling overwhelmed by big emotions. Create a list of smaller goals for daily rewards and bigger ones for monthly prizes. You'll be motivated to work toward them for sure.

Exercise 61

Board games can help you build patience.

https://www.pexels.com/photo/close-up-photo-of-monopoly-board-game-776654/

Another way to build patience and resist impulsive behavior is by playing games where players must wait for their turn. Play board games with your family as often as possible, and you'll see your patience improve. You'll get frustrated less often and develop better impulse control.

Section 7: Plan like a Pro

Children with ADHD need some help with planning. Planning effectively means understanding how to organize, prioritize tasks, and manage your time. Do you have trouble deciding how long something will take you to complete, or do you *procrastinate* (wait and wait and wait) and end up being late all the time? If yes, you have poor time management skills. Likewise, if you tend to start many tasks at a time but have trouble deciding which ones to do first, you don't know how to *prioritize*. If you do tasks out of order, differently for no reason, you may have poor *organizational skills*. Luckily, practice makes perfect.

Children with ADHD need some help with planning.

Exercise 62

Learning how to become a regular planner is more a practice than an exercise - but it's the first step in building powerful planning skills.

Instructions:

1. Get a calendar and mark important tasks and dates on it.
2. Use a checklist for tasks without a set due date.
3. Create reminders for deadlines.
4. Break large tasks into smaller ones.
5. Include the small tasks into your daily schedule to ensure they'll get done.
6. Write a to-do list every weekend for the next month.
7. Have clear goals - both smaller and larger goals can motivate you.

At the end of the month, look at the tasks you got done and the ones you didn't. What kept you from completing them all?

Exercise 63

The Watch Out for the Mistakes activity has the following rules:

- Don't start working on goals without a strategy for accomplishing every task, or you'll get distracted and fail to complete them.
- Don't plan everything out in tiny details as plans change; if you expect to stick to plans that aren't working, you'll get frustrated.
- Don't forget to think about why you set a particular goal.
- If you notice you started procrastinating, make up the lost time as soon as possible.
- Instead of panicking if you need to change the plan, pivot and think of other ways to continue working toward your goal.
- Don't spend all your time planning; make sure you stay on track by *actually doing the work*!

Exercise 64

The SMART goal method is an excellent way to get into the habit of *prioritizing* - deciding which tasks must be completed right away and which can wait. For example, between a school project due in two days and a test in two weeks, *the project comes first.* Why? Because it is due sooner. SMART goals work for people with ADHD because they motivate them to plan better.

SMART stands for:

- **S**pecific (be clear about the target)
- **M**easurable (you need to track your success)
- **A**ttainable (you know for sure you can do it within the given time frame)
- **R**elevant (you gain something by achieving it)
- **T**ime-Limited (there is a due date)

When setting SMART goals, have regular checkup points to stop and look at your progress. It will motivate you to stay on track and complete your plan.

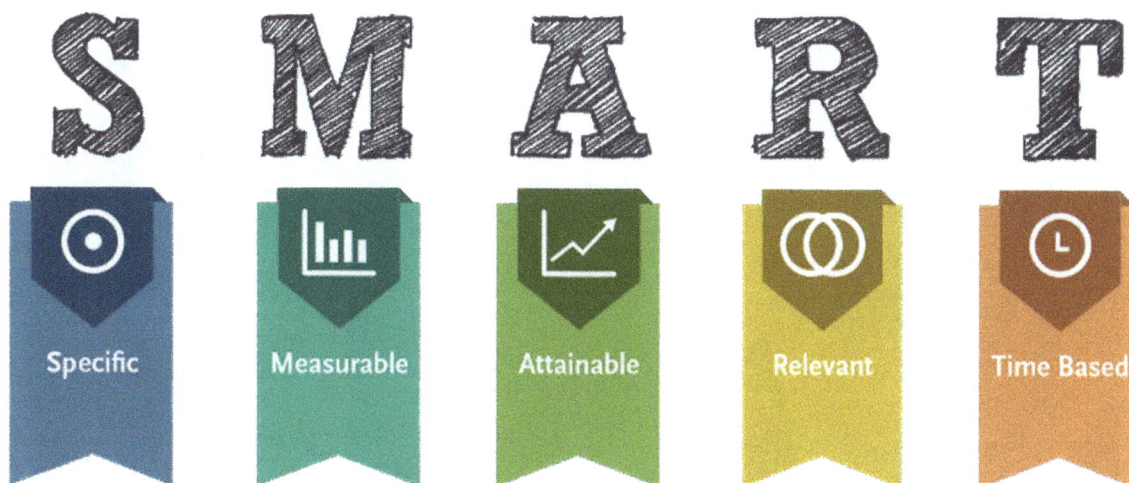

When setting SMART goals, have regular checkup points to stop and look at your progress.
Dungdm93, CC BY-SA 4.0 <https://creativecommons.org/licenses/by-sa/4.0>, via Wikimedia Commons:
https://commons.wikimedia.org/wiki/File:SMART-goals.png

Exercise 65

Cooking is a fantastic way to learn planning skills. Following recipes requires time management, preparing the ingredients tests your organization skills, and doing the steps in the correct order. This is a super example of *prioritization*. Cooking can be as simple as putting a salad together or making a smoothie. Find a recipe you like, hunt down the ingredients, and prepare them as described in the instructions.

Exercise 66

How many times have you gotten frustrated because you planned to do something but didn't tell your parents, and they had other plans? To avoid this, make it a habit of letting your plans be known as soon as you make them. Each morning, tell your parents what you have planned for the day. Communicating your plans makes it more likely you'll stick to them.

Exercise 67

The *Park Obstacle* game requires you to plan your route through an imaginary park while avoiding obstacles. On small pieces of paper, write down the different obstacles like rocks, trees, dogs, buildings, etc. You can walk beside some obstacles (rocks, for example), while dogs or trees should be avoided at a greater distance. Cover the table with green craft paper to represent the park. Ask someone to determine where the obstacles will be and place them on the green paper. Now, it's up to you to plan how to get from one end of the park to another.

Exercise 68

How Much Time Does it Take is an activity that helps you organize your schedule based on the time it takes to do the activities included. In a large piece of paper (or in a planner app on the phone), set a detailed timing grid in 5-minute increments. Create a list of your activities and put everything into the grid by estimating how much it takes you to do it. For example, you can calculate how long it takes you to organize your school bag and materials. Then, you'll know whether the task is something you should do in the morning or the evening.

Exercise 69

Gardening can help you plan.
https://www.pexels.com/photo/women-gardening-5529587/

If you have a garden, you can see how much planning goes into planting your flowers or vegetables. Get an adult to help you determine which plants should go where. For example, some plants don't like shade, so they should go to a sunny spot. You'll need to pay attention to how your garden looks and how much space you have and plan accordingly. If you're planting similar flowers, think about what colors go together and plan their placement to make the best color matches.

Exercise 70

The "What Do I Do First?" is an exercise of prioritization skills. Imagine you have five hours between arriving home from school and going to bed. Here is what you need to do during this time:

- Meet friends
- Wash up
- Have dinner
- Change clothes
- Do homework for tomorrow
- Work on assignment due in a week
- Play on your phone or computer
- Prepare for bed
- Pack your school bag for the next day

In what order should you do all these tasks?

WHAT DO I DO FIRST?

○ _____

○ _____

○ _____

○ _____

○ _____

○ _____

○ _____

○ _____

○ _____

○ _____

Exercise 71

Do you have a favorite motivational quote you would like to display in your room? Figure out where to place it and see how much space you have for it. Write your motivational quote, making sure you have enough room for all the words first! Or, if you're good with a computer, design it with a digital program.

Section 8: Social Skills and Self-Esteem

With ADHD, you may find managing your emotions challenging when socializing with big groups. You may lose confidence and find it hard to make friends. Fortunately, working on your social skills can boost your self-esteem. One of the main parts of learning social skills is reading *social cues* -hints about what's really going on with people!

One of the fundamental aspects of learning social skills is reading social cues.
https://pixabay.com/vectors/argument-couple-disagreement-female-2022605/

Social cues are a form of non-verbal communication between people. For example, you might notice that your classmate gets upset about something you said by seeing them frowning and turning away. They might not say they're upset, but those hints tell you to ask them what's wrong. Or, another friend might smile at you, communicating without words that they want to play with you.

Beyond these examples, social cues can be divided into four categories:

- **Facial expressions:** Frowning, smiling, puzzling, neutral, etc.

Social cues are a form of non-verbal communication between people.
https://www.pexels.com/photo/collage-of-portraits-of-cheerful-woman-3807758/

- **Personal space:** Stepping closer or farther away from others indicates personal comfort level.

- **Vocal pitch:** How their voice sounds can be high or low – or in-between – and this can tell you more about what someone means to say. For example, if they say hello in a low voice with their head down, this means they aren't excited to see you. Something may be bothering them.

- **Body language:** Slumping, straight posture, crossing arms, turning away, etc.

These hints (*cues*) help you figure out what others think and feel; that way, you can react properly in different situations. If you miss social cues, you can create misunderstandings, which will affect your relationships.

Exercise 72

Learning to read nonverbal cues is a great way to improve your social skills. Here are some tips on what to look for:

- **Listen to someone speak.** Are they alternating between a high and a low-pitched voice? If yes, they're probably trying to communicate something important.

Listen to someone speak.
https://pixabay.com/vectors/sound-listening-man-ear-hearing-159915/

- If they emphasize words by speaking them more loudly, this is the information you should listen to.

- If they're talking fast, they're probably nervous; if they're talking slowly, they're relaxed and confident.

- Do they make long pauses and turn toward you while they speak? If yes, they're waiting for you to respond.

- Are the facial expressions welcoming (like a smile, open eyes, etc.) or not (frowning, raising eyebrows)?

- Do they look into your eyes or in other directions? When someone is interested in talking to you, they'll look into your eyes more frequently.

- Are they standing close, turned toward you with their body, or are halfway turned away - this is a clear signal they aren't interested.

- Do they use welcoming gestures like moving their arms openly by their sides or negative ones like shaking their heads or shrugging?

Exercise 73

Silent Snack is a voiceless communication game relying entirely on social cues. Gather friends or family and place several snacks into individual bowls. Place the bowls on the table and ask everyone to stop talking during the game. The players should exchange snack bowls and share their opinions of the snack using only gestures, facial expressions, and body language.

Exercise 74

The classic *Charades* game can help you read and practice nonverbal cues. Gather your fellow players and choose the scenarios, people, or animals you want to act out. Include emotions (like sadness, fear, boredom, wariness, pride, happiness, etc.), too. As you play this game, you'll build plenty of social skills and raise your confidence when using them.

Exercise 75

You can also learn nonverbal cues from movies. Watch your favorite movie for 10 minutes. Stop it and think about what nonverbal cues you've seen. Did these cues help you understand what's going on in the movie? Were you confused about some of them? If so, ask your parents what those cues mean.

Exercise 76

Start with yourself! Think about how you act in certain situations. How do you convey with your nonverbal cues that you are:

Surprised o———————————————————————————————
———————————————————————————————————

Disappointed o————————————————————————————
———————————————————————————————————

Confused o———————————————————————————————
———————————————————————————————————

Sad o———————————————————————————————————
———————————————————————————————————

Angry o———————————————————————————————————
———————————————————————————————————

Nervous o—————————————————————————————————
———————————————————————————————————

Anxious o—————————————————————————————————
———————————————————————————————————

Proud o———————————————————————————————————
———————————————————————————————————

Start observing others. Do you notice them using the same cues as you to convey the same feelings and thoughts?

Exercise 77

Building confidence is easy with the *Ladder of Achievements* exercise. Think about a skill you want to improve - this should be a skill you can measure and track its progress. For example, if you have trouble sitting without fidgeting for longer than 10 minutes, make it a goal to sit still for 12 minutes. When you can do that, increase the time.

Exercise 78

Another self-esteem-boosting exercise is communicating as if you were your pet. Ask a friend with pets to start a *pet pen pal* with you. This works great if you have trouble communicating directly with this friend. You'll be less intimidated if you write from your pet's perspective instead of your own.

Exercise 79

The *Optimist* game helps you build a positive self-image. It's great for families where everyone can participate to create a positive atmosphere. Write down everyone's names on a piece of paper, and ask everyone to say something nice to each other, about something that makes them happy, etc. The more positive you sound, the better you'll feel about yourself!

Exercise 80

Is there something new you want to try or an old hobby you left behind because you thought you weren't good at it? Finding activities you enjoy and using your talents can be a huge confidence booster. Create a list of these activities and ask your parents for suggestions if you don't know where to start. Aim for low difficulty levels first, and create a plan to reach higher levels; this will boost your motivation.

Exercise 81

The *Resilience Roadmap* teaches you about your strengths so you can take pride in yourself. Connect negative experiences like having an activity canceled, getting into an argument with a friend, failing to achieve a goal, being mistreated, etc., with positive reactions.

Section 9: Bringing It All Together

As its name implies, this section combines all the necessary skills in one place and offers you ten more exercises to practice these skills.

Exercise 82

The *Storybook* game can improve your attention, memory, and organizational skills. All you need is your favorite book, a piece of paper, and someone to write a couple of questions about what you'll read. Questions can include:

- Who is the main character?
- What does (the character's name) do when they get to (a location described in a story)?
- What do you think of their actions?
- What would you have done in their place?

Exercise 83

As an alternative to the previous activity, read a couple of paragraphs from a book you're reading for the first time and try to guess how the story will unfold. You'll need to remember what you've read previously to stay close to the original story, but use your imagination (and planning skills) to come up with what could happen next. Read the story for a few minutes again. Then, compare the original story to what you came up with. Go back and forth a couple of times like this to boost your concentration, logic, and working memory.

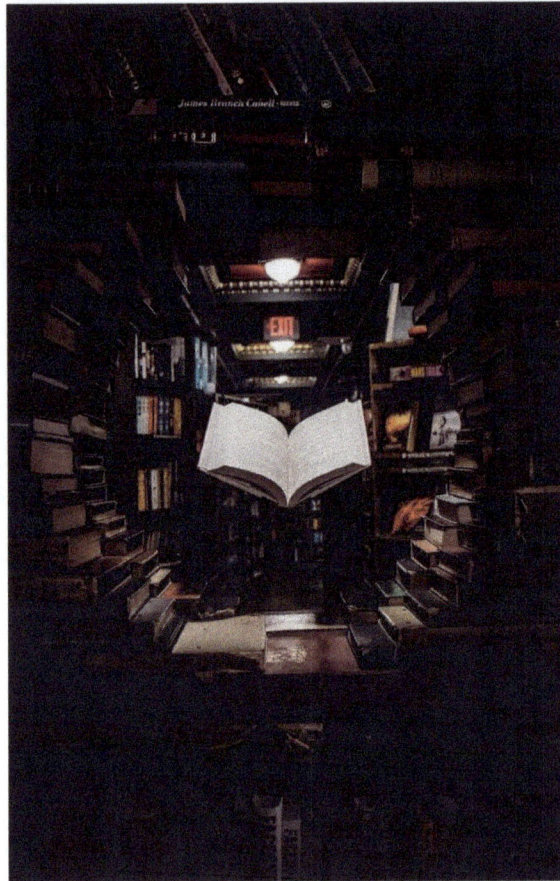

Read a couple of paragraphs from a book you're reading for the first time and try to guess how the story will unfold.

Exercise 84

Going to the zoo is always a fun experience - and even more so if you spruce it up with a game. Invite whoever is going for a *Spying Animals* challenge. Everyone writes down the names of as many animals as they can. When you get to the zoo, everyone tries to spot as many creatures as possible from their list.

Exercise 85

The *Daily Motivational Awareness* practice requires you to find motivation to face your challenges. Do this every day when you wake up. Does knowing you'll see your friends at school inspire you to go to school even though you know you'll struggle with keeping up during the classes? Write down any other motivations you can think of. If you can't come up with anything in the morning, do it in the evening - you'll be able to remember what made it easier to get through challenging situations during that day.

Exercise 86

Until now, you had plenty of exercises to help you uncover your strengths. Now, think about an activity that tests them, like sitting still in a classroom, taking a test, or watching a movie with your family. Pick the top five powers that you know for sure will come in handy, then answer the following question for each one:

- How do I use this strength during this activity?

- How will using this strength help me?

- Can I use it in a different, better way?

- Is there a plan, and if so, when will the power come in handy?

- Can/should the same strength be used several times?

- What happens if the ability helps me meet my goals?

Exercise 87

The activity *I Saw* is a great way to sharpen your focus. You can play it anytime, anywhere, and you don't need any supplies. For example, when traveling by car or bus, pay attention to how many different colored cars you see traveling on the road. When you get home, try to remember and write down how many red, blue, and black cars you saw.

Exercise 88

This *Progressive Muscle Relaxation* exercise will help you improve all your executive functioning skills. Here is how to do it:

1. Stand straight, and imagine you're a cat that just woke up from its sleep, ready to strengthen your limbs.

2. Stretch your arms in front of you, lift them over your head, then let them fall to your side.

3. Lift your shoulders so your ears touch them, then strengthen your neck.

4. Bite down hard on your teeth, then relax your jaw.

5. Wrinkle your nose and then relax your face.

6. Make your stomach tight, as hard as you feel it is when you feel anxious, and release.

7. Press your feet to the floor like you're squeezing your toes into a muddy puddle, and relax your legs.

8. Finally, let your body go limp as if you're a ragdoll.

Do you feel relaxed? Whatever you do later, your focus and attention will be sharper.

Exercise 89

During the *Tree Day Focus* exercise, you'll pay attention to any positive experience you have in your life. This could be successfully avoiding getting distracted, remaining calm when facing big emotions, sticking to a plan, or any other victory you had. The experience or memory represents the root of a tree, while the positive feelings it led to represents its branches. Write these down in a journal in detail (use that working memory) and think about the positive feelings they evoked.

Exercise 90

The *End of the Word and the Beginning of the Next* is a fun group activity you can play anywhere to kill time. It improves your communication, attention, and executive functioning skills. One player says a word, and the next person must listen to it and then say a new word that starts with the last letter of the previous one.

Exercise 91

Find the way from one end of the maze to the other.

This exercise will test your attention, planning, and creative thinking skills.

Find the way from one end of the maze to the other. Do your best to avoid getting distracted; don't look far ahead or backward.

Was this challenging? Did you notice how the picture looked like a spiral? What helped you break through the illusion and remain focused on finding the way out?

Bonus Activities: Optical Illusions

The following optical illusion exercises aim to enhance your ability to focus, concentrate, and be mindful while improving your ability to spot small details.

Exercise 92

Can you *Spot the Hidden Dog?* is a classic brain teaser that improves your attention to detail as it makes you look hard at the picture.

There's a dog hidden here. Can you spot it?

Did you find the dog? How long did it take you to find it? Was it easy for you to find the doggy from the cats?

Exercise 93

Do the rails have the same length?

https://pixabay.com/vectors/railroad-track-rail-transportation-1587328/

Look at the horizontal (going left to right) in the picture. Are they all the same length?

(How long did it take to figure out they are the same length, even if the ones further away seem bigger? Were you able to tell right away they're the same length?)

Exercise 94

Look at the picture. Are the horizontal lines level? Or are they slanted?

Was it challenging to see the lines are straight? Did the differences in the square pattern make it hard to tell?

Exercise 95

Find craft paper in several shades of the same color. Cut out equal-sized strips and place them beside each other, beginning from the darkest and finishing with the lightest. Take a closer look at the strips. Is each one made of a solid block of color?

Did it seem that when placed beside each other, the strips suddenly have different color variations in them? Were you fooled by the optical illusion of thinking the strips have darker and lighter elements?

Exercise 96

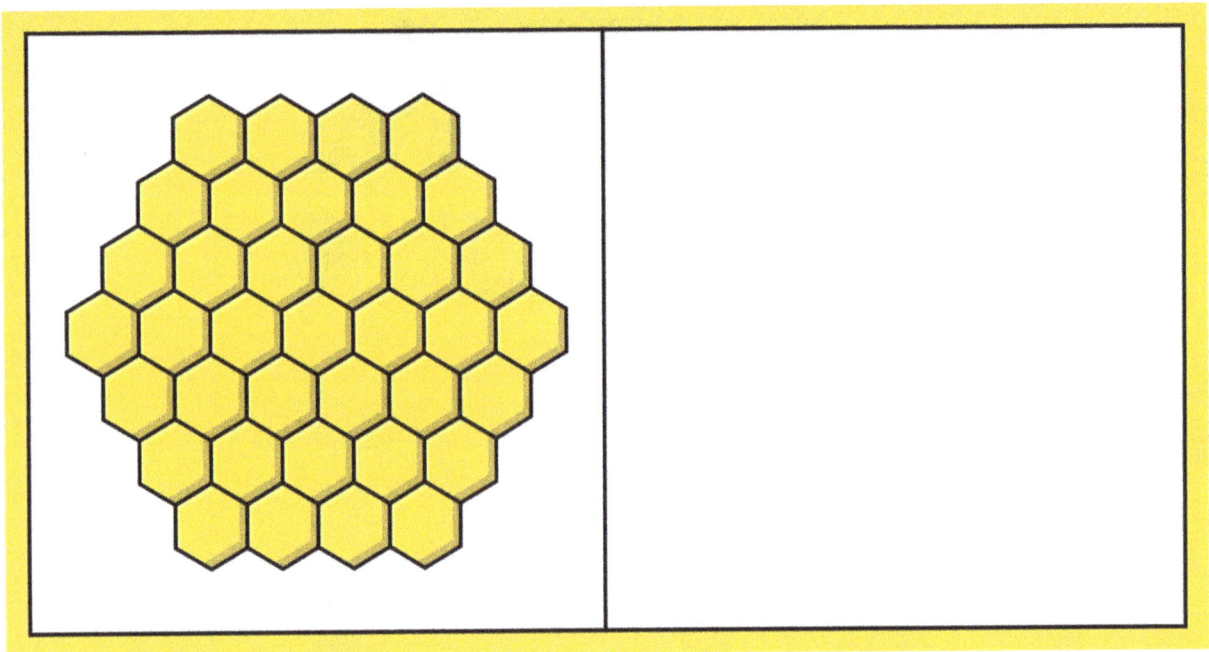

Try to replicate the pattern from the first box on the empty one. Pay close attention to all the lines and how they're depicted in the picture.

Were you able to draw the pattern that looks like the picture? Or did you have trouble following the lines and make some errors?

Draw two large circles about a finger width apart from each other. Connect them with two lines. Create two small squares in front of the first and after the second circle at the same height as the lines between. In the first circle, draw or place a sticker of a bird. In the second, draw a cage slightly bigger than the bird. Cut out the circles but keep them attached in the middle (cut following the two lines there), and keep the small circles attached to them. Fold the shape in the middle of the two lines and glue the two circles together with the picture on the outside. They should now have a small square on both sides. Create a hole and tug a string through both squares. Start twisting the strings, then pull them sharply upwards. The circles will start spinning rapidly.

Did you notice how the bird appeared inside the cage as the two images seemed to blend?

Can you spy with your eye on all the items that aren't animals?

Can you spy with your eye on all the items that aren't animals? Color them.

Did you find them all and leave the animals black and white?

Exercise 99

Starting from a middle point, draw 8 curvy lines, creating 4 curvy "roads" that meet in the middle. Connect the outside lines of the roads with two smaller stripes like you're drawing several large circles or spirals between the roads. Write the word twinkle on all four roads, taking up all the space with double-lined letters. Color the letters and the inside of every second circle intercepting the roads yellow. Color the other circles and the space around the letters green.

Exercise 100

Draw an outline of an egg on white paper. Draw lines across the paper (including the egg). Keep your lines straight above, below, and beside the egg. However, when a line reaches the inside of the egg's outline, draw it in a way so it follows the egg's shape. Make the stripes within the egg curve upward at the top and downwards at the bottom. Color the space between two lines a different color across the entire paper. Inside the egg, add small shapes between the lines to decorate the egg.

Look at the picture.

Did you notice how the lines outside the egg appear slightly curvy? What do you think of this optical illusion?

Exercise 101

Can you guess the animals by their shadows?

https://pixabay.com/vectors/animal-bear-collection-silhouettes-1297864/

Can you guess the animals by their shadows? Did you find it hard to match the illusion with the real animal?

Thank You

Thank you for taking the time to complete this brain training book. Besides learning about your condition, you now have plenty of tools to bring positive changes into your life. Hopefully, you found the activities engaging enough to work hard and have gained new and empowering skills to overcome your challenges. Now, you have a treasure chest full of abilities and strategies to use when you feel overwhelmed and unable to focus. Congratulations on being one step closer to your dream of living a happy, productive life. Thank you for unlocking your power!

Check out another book in the series

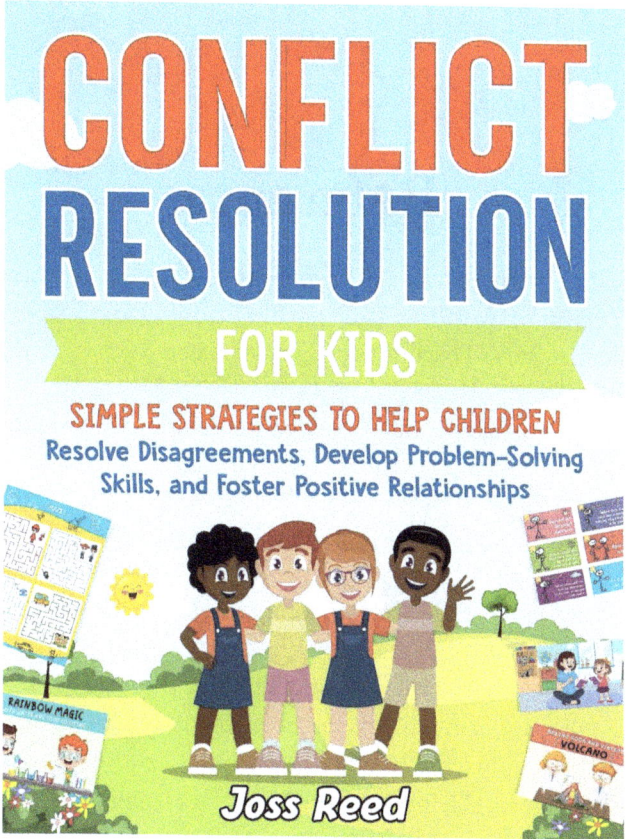

References

10-Minute Strategies To Teach Planning Skills. (2023, May 16). Life Skills Advocate. https://lifeskillsadvocate.com/blog/10-minute-strategies-to-teach-planning-skills/

51 Top "Optical Illusions Worksheets" Teaching Resources curated for you. (n.d.). Twinkl. https://www.twinkl.com/search?q=optical+illusions+worksheets&c=249&r=parent

585 Top "Memory Activities" Teaching Resources curated for you. (n.d.). Twinkl. https://www.twinkl.com/search?q=memory+activities&c=249&ct=Other&r=parent

ADHD. (n.d.). Kidshealth.Org. https://kidshealth.org/en/kids/adhdkid.html#:~:text=ADHD%20is%20a%20medical%20condition,and%20get%20into%20trouble%20more.

Attention-Deficit / Hyperactivity Disorder (ADHD) in Children. (n.d.). Hopkinsmedicine.Org. https://www.hopkinsmedicine.org/health/conditions-and-diseases/adhdadd

Avoid These Top 5 Planning Mistakes. (n.d.). Leanoutmethod.Com. https://www.leanoutmethod.com/blog/avoid-these-top-5-planning-mistakes

Be Mindful to Stress Less. (n.d.). Kidshealth.Org. https://kidshealth.org/en/kids/mindfulness.html

Burch, K. (n.d.). What Are Benefits of Having ADHD? Verywell Health. https://www.verywellhealth.com/benefits-of-adhd-strengths-and-superpowers-5210520

Chris Hanson. (2020, July 23). 10 Planning Skills Every Child Should Learn. Life Skills Advocate. https://lifeskillsadvocate.com/blog/10-planning-skills-every-child-should-learn/

Courtney E. Ackerman, M. A. (2019, May 27). 49 Communication Activities, Exercises & Games. PositivePsychology.Com. https://positivepsychology.com/communication-games-and-activities/

Elaine Houston, B. S. (2019, September 30). 19 Top Positive Psychology Exercises for Clients or Students. PositivePsychology.Com. https://positivepsychology.com/positive-psychology-exercises/

Forbes Coaches Council. (2017, October 18). Look Before You Leap: 17 Ways To Slow Down Impulsive Decisions. Forbes. htfps://www.forbes.com/sites/forbescoachescouncil/2017/10/18/look-before-you-leap-17-ways-to-slow-down-impulsive-decisions/?sh=525af08b4440

Games, M. E. (2020, August 24). The Best Games for ADHD Kids. MentalUP.Co; MentalUP. https://www.mentalup.co/blog/attention-games-for-adhd

Goally. (2023, May 31). How to Control Impulsive Behavior In a Child. Goalie Apps & Tablets for Kids. https://getgoally.com/blog/how-to-control-impulsive-behavior-in-a-child/

Illusions and mind tricks: are your eyes fooling you? (n.d.). TheSchoolRun. https://www.theschoolrun.com/illusions-and-mind-tricks-are-your-eyes-fooling-you

Kristin McCarthy, M. E., & More, R. (2021, December 16). 41 Learning Quotes for Kids to Get Them Excited & Motivated. LoveToKnow. https://www.lovetoknow.com/quotes-quips/inspirational/41-learning-quotes-kids-get-them-excited-motivated

Low, K. (n.d.). Using Your Memory With ADD as a Therapeutic Strategy. Verywell mind. https://www.verywellmind.com/add-and-working-memory-20796

Myers, R. (2008, June 24). 10 Concentration and Focus Building Techniques for Children with ADHD. Empowering Parents. https://www.empoweringparents.com/article/5-simple-concentration-building-techniques-for-kids-with-adhd/

NeuronUP. (2021, July 13). 5 activities designed to work with children with ADHD. Neuronup.Us. https://neuronup.us/neurorehabilitation-activities/activities-for-adhd/5-activities-designed-to-work-with-children-with-adhd/

Sandoval, W. (2021, October 5). ADHD Brain Training: How It Works, Exercises & Tech. Healthline. https://www.healthline.com/health/adhd/adhd-brain-training

Shakibaie, S. (2021, March 31). 10 Activities That Are Good for ADHD Children. Ready Kids. https://readykids.com.au/10-activities-that-are-good-for-adhd-children/

Sutton, J. (2022, February 4). How to Read Nonverbal Communication Cues: 5 Techniques. PositivePsychology.Com. https://positivepsychology.com/nonverbal-communication-cues/

Talking with Your Child About ADHD. (2018, May 8). CHADD. https://chadd.org/adhd-weekly/talking-with-your-child-about-adhd/

Watson, S. (2021, February 8). 21 Ways to Make Lemonade During the Sourest Times. ADDitude. https://www.additudemag.com/activities-for-kids-with-adhd-skills-pandemic/

Wright, L. W. (2019, August 5). Types of Social Cues. Understood. https://www.understood.org/en/articles/4-types-of-social-cues

www.ingramcontent.com/pod-product-compliance
Lightning Source LLC
Chambersburg PA
CBHW050013110426
42741CB00038B/3412